God's Laughter

La Croix

Presentation by *BookLeaf Publishing*

Web: www.bookleafpub.com

E-mail: info@bookleafpub.com

ISBN: 9789357441643

First edition 2023

PSALM 23:4

PSALM 23:4
"Even though I walk through the valley of the shadow of death, I fear no evil, for You are with me; Your rod and Your staff, they comfort me."

If one more person tells me to be Strong, Im going to break their legs Mafia style and tell them to walk it off.
There's no Strong in this moment- I'm weak as I watch my son's body carried by grown men, as my husband cries, and as I have to explain to his sister why her brother is in the hospital.
I want the pain and fear to engulf me. I want to submit to the higher power and be still in my weakness.
So still that maybe this moment wont notice me or my son.

ROMANS 8:28

ROMANS 8:28
"God promises to make something good out of the storms that bring devastation to your life."

The Gift of Health isn't found in a Tiffany Blue box.
Christmas is two weeks away and I want what I cant shop for- my son to be healthy right now.
Health is the best Gift.

JEREMIAH 29:11

JEREMIAH 29:11
"For I know the plans I have for you ... plans to prosper you and not to harm you, plans to give you hope and a future."

The Chaplain is a Black Queer women from Brooklyn.
She made sure I took care of myself my mentioning the double billing Id receive from the Children's and Adult hospital.
But she also centered me by letting me know that the I'm waiting on the "Big Reveal" and God doesn't work that way.

ECCLESIASTES 7:9

ECCLESIASTES 7:9
"Be not quick in your spirit to become angry, for anger lodges in the heart of fools."

Screaming in your car in either directions between the hospital and home while loudly playing afro-beats is self-care.

MATTHEW 11:28

MATTHEW 11:28
"Come to me, all who labor and are heavy laden,
and I will give you rest."

Pieces
Laying on the floor in a hospital chapel with
tears dripping into my ears.
Peace

ROMANS 12:15

ROMANS 12:15
"Be happy with those who are happy, and cry
with those who are crying."

500+ Linkedin contacts
200+ FB

Yet I can only list 6ppl on the visitor list.
I think God for this number as it protected us
from those that just want to "come see" the car
crush of my life not provide a shoulder to lean
on.

ROMANS 8:28

ROMANS 8:28
"God promises to make something good out of
the storms that bring devastation to your life."

My Sister inLaw makes great Lasagna. It wasn't
until today that I realize what feeding people
that are going through a hard time mean. I had
been on the cooking not receiving time for so
long....a hot meal that you didn't make is LOVE.

PROVERBS 22:6

PROVERBS 22:6
"Train up a child in the way he should go, and
when he is old, he will not depart from it."

They've taken so much blood from my little guy-
test upon test for everything internal. He does
deep breathing as the needle puncture his veins.
This technique I taught both of my kids to center
themselves he remembers. Not his name but
how to be brave by breathing.

MATTHEW 17:20

MATTHEW 17:20
"Our faith can move mountains."

Pray circles around the world are keeping me
sane.

ISAIAH 66:13

ISAIAH 66:13
"As a mother comforts her child, so I will comfort you; in Jerusalem you shall find your comfort."

My mother is here in my home...taking care of her child (me) as I take care of mine.

2 TIMOTHY 4:17

2 TIMOTHY 4:17
"But the Lord stood with me and gave me strength."

My husband Prayed for the best Hospital and Best Staff. The great spirit heard him, we have had the best people with such hearts for our son's well being.

1 PETER 5:7

1 PETER 5:7
"Cast all your anxiety on him because he cares for you."

The Chaplain saved my life every time that she checked in on me and didn't mentioned one time to be strong.

ISAIAH 40:29

ISAIAH 40:29
"He gives power to the weak and strength to the powerless."

Funny not Funny- everyone referred to me as "MOM" as my son was in a medical coma, and not once did I feel erased.

PSALM 30:11

PSALM 30:11
"You have turned for me my mourning into
dancing; you have loosed my sackcloth and
clothed me with gladness."

A Black nurse named Angela diagnose our son.
Every milestone he makes I whisper her name in
thanks.

2 CORINTHIANS 5:7

2 CORINTHIANS 5:7
"For we walk by faith, not by sight."

Hubby and I are of one single mind regarding the care and recovery of our son. The voice of direction talks to both of us clearly.

ROMANS 12:9

ROMANS 12:9
"Let love be genuine. Abhor what is evil; hold
fast to what is good."

Nothing like your Mother in Law who barely
has access to her son much less her grandkids
saying " My God will punish you (her son), and
your wife for keeping me from my grandkids."
as your son is in the rehab part of CHOA and
you're both haven't slept in days.

PSALM 23:1

PSALM 23:1
"The LORD is my shepherd, I lack nothing."

Thankfully for GREAT Healthcare. So, so
Thankful.

DEUTERONOMY 31:6

DEUTERONOMY 31:6
"Be strong and courageous. Do not be afraid or terrified because of them, for the LORD your God goes with you; he will never leave you nor forsake you."

36 days of horror. 36 days of not sleeping on the same bed as my hubby. 36 days of the worst feeling ever- not knowing if your son is Healthy or not.
And it just the beginning.
To the Me on the other side of this- He made it back to us better and Healthier than ever.
Thankful for my children.

www.ingramcontent.com/pod-product-compliance
Lightning Source LLC
La Vergne TN
LVHW050312210726
843507LV00020B/3107